I0159257

In The Arms of the Honey Eaters

Anon Edition

2013

Los Angeles

IN THE ARMS
OF THE
HONEY EATERS

+ + + + + + + + + + + +

Selected Writing

Jhim Pattison

ISBN 978-0-9761436-0-4 (cloth)
978-0-9761436-3-5 (paper)

Now that those who hold our roads
Night priests,
Have come out standing to their sacred place,
We have passed you on your roads.

Our daylight fathers,
Our daylight mothers,
After so many days,
Eight days,
On the ninth day you will copulate with rams.

(Koyemshi prayer)

+   +   +   +   +   +   +   +

One of the most impressive Greek rites was a pilgrimage along the Sacred Way Iron Athens to Eleusis. The route was lined with temples, and sacrifices were made and hymns sung. At one point along the way a man called a "bridger," because he sat on the bridge of the river Kephissos, hurled obscene jests and curses at the pilgrims. Like the Pueblo clowns, he was officially sanctioned, or one might say, required.

ADIOS

Marry me!

Ever since I've been a drummer, on the couch,

in a nutshell, with the little fighting babies

tugging in a dialect beknownst to thee.

Where's the blind door one crawls towards?

The garden shadows wet, sky a distant black cavern,

invisible fingers printing with fire

an emerald oak, recombinant time machine

of gamelan chess parts near the cold invisible lake

secreting the silver of diaphanous night

The candles lit

Released back into the forest

The plank between worlds disseminated

to speak in the tonal pillars of known alchemies

I assassinate your disregard for an enchanted life

for an angry concordance in the lovers' wind circle

A true passion of the assassin

waxing in the sharp flint of lost rain

The candles were lit

with the skin of other suns

the aroma of quicksilver and cherry

ATTAWP / ATTONCE / POKATOWER

bow   arrow   fire

The Moon in the Man

to Schlechter Duvall

When I lived gentle with the manatee fluid, three mermaids
were kneeling on a rock kissing my hunter-goddess with
spine. Our shoulders were harps while I & those I choose to
love invent the tangram our hearts were built to be. This
woman, carol of our dialog, the only woman we will ever feel,
time-traveler in the Philosophy of Religious Mathematics
connecting the cobra with herself. There's a kiss, the last kiss
of childhood, mentioned by this woman we love, in league
with our periphery of shields, the other mirror image of the
ingrown trombone careless amongst human flesh, a night-bird
upon Perseus' blade, corymbos alive as I count coup when
entering the lonely prehistoric sea.

Lovely prehistoric coral where perhaps I dreamed a mythos
speaking in aging tongues dancing near the keys on monkey
flames, in labyrinth, in honeycombs, and you are the salt of
the Ocean; beware lonely prehistoric sea.

seer

seer

seer

seer

seer

seer

seer

seer

seer

seer

seer

seer

seer

seer

seer

seer

seer

You as the seer say you've met that eye

seer

seer

seer   of the ancient toll

seer

seer

Where my wolves are a lure to a mirror of snow

With the stolen night on the tips of your hands
and holding the day with marionette eyes
A compass that weaves intermissions behind
                    honey-birds of the heart
and calls like your lips of the moon

I must open the magnets before they are
                    empty glass

With all the combinations to unlock the ocean's pulse
I have met a woman so beautiful
That I hold the tickets for her
                    afternoons at night
In me she has made language move
and given the hypnotic eclipse its pillow
as the wind rises from the flame. . . .

Tomorrow now and never in the tearing nest
                    of roses
We have become lighter than air and lifted by the jewel
umbrella
and our will is alone in the parallels
and I am inside the witness to your perfume of gallant feathers

Hand me the garden and we will swim across the mysterious
harps

1 - 1

The blazing curtain has become a shadow
through the crystal fan of your eyes
traversing the mantle in a violet limb.
You will not return remorseless
from the resonance of my copra.
But on the golden meal whispering
smoke behind the sheath of fine chills
will you connect a rainbow to the
canals of my sunken ears.
Again the plows of fluid hands demand
curds of fragrant dance wounds
immersed in the spirit of heathen sap.
You have nailed the key of freedom to the
wall of chance with a sleeping kick
to the heart of the invisible hostess
licking my abdomen with her will.

1 - - 1

Corollaries harmonic
with steel drums sift the plums from
my dream of unknown beasts
that tickle the corners of your teeth.
I say unknown but analogy offers
The cheer of refound services
These crawlers have anonymously
touched with their
oneirays of flesh whips in violent
randomness as instinct prefers.
At all spaces. In every leaf of
birth. Through the icons of
abortive space. Lips of mold, take care!
You have become the earth, nothing
less, insurgent wing!
An amourous buoy rigs magneticized
goblets pushed by arcing serpents
                    serpentine arcs

To A Greater Love

for Mwaure

Ice is heard falling from an echoed plume
    where language belongs to knives
A shore apart from a wind of emblems
We enfold in our breathing blood
the chorus of fantom wheels and agates
I am asking for a direct freedom for you
    when our eyes begin the sentence alone
At a great distance
Orchards pulled from a gloved flame
Endure nothing more than kilts of science
    and our houses burn for more than one
reason

At the opening of your temple I inject a quest

I ask only for a trail of whispers

on the dress of a falcon

Where you have become the rain sirens in the anthem sign

and the vines of blood memory

In the camelias that shed scent amid the opal dancers

in the green crystals of volcanic light

I ask for reciprocal love alone prepared

That total magnetization over which

Nothing can power and which makes

Flesh into sun

I wait for the kiss of your soft red wings

with the heart-map you've cast into my

eyes

Over these lagoons and caverns with the shouting arrows

My hands see your beautiful blue ocelot

drink from the founted window

You not only laugh the cry of the nebula gown

But walk next to me in the curtains

                         tying our wind among the dragons

The Ascent of Mary W. Shelley

for Laurence Weisberg
& it's double

There is a jaguar among us
masked in igloos with the pageant of blood cycles
where I mermaid the tradition of heart-skulls
Dreaming gold of shadow, moons are hurled
from your wings of fire gardenias
into a night-flood chanting the Yoruba light
when we are the constellation of raven flesh

There is a jaguar among us
whose mating call is the temper of owl-quartz
whose vision is of a nest of ghosts
The golden pelican frozen into touch
The tribal juices kissing like love under the yellow jackets
with a magnificence of fins

From the sacrificial drink in the first chorus of language

I am bleeding from an ancient wound

Knives before water *clasp our violin hands*

north of the zodiac with its magma arrows

with its houri of rose anatomy with a bird's memory

and a calculus of tears there is a jaguar among us

in the mystery of handshakes at twilight

Strange Destiny

I.

The Inherited Bride shadows on the moon
   Serpentine Falcon's lair
The hour that changes (the world)
the velvet glove aerobics peace of mind
The Realms Of Gold

II.

Golden Totem Golden Totem,
Secret kingdom, be my guest
Vanishing bride, the luckiest girl in (the world)
Honey badger for love of a pagan
holiday for love, orphan of the shadows, emeralds in the dark –
Getaway, The Romantic Spirit – a Venice in the dark Edge of
violence bound by honor coma
Winterwood

Grand Deception

Prayers that are answered:

Who gets the drumstick?, brave new world, gather then the

rose

the Moonflower vine a strange elation, circle of love,

Amazing love,

Full circle

Running along the sapphire river law of the owl symphony
pulled through belladonna gateways, bursts of cryptic amnesia
in the flowering library of apparitions, the vanishing cul-de-sac
of misshapen lunacy, the discovery of wind
Hollow wind, delirious wind, a silhouette of sleep

Running beneath the myelitic river law of the owl espionage
in an exiled memory struck by lightning (switches)
a shift in the dance pharmacopoeia
They see you and you won't know who they are
in a cocktail of elements, a blue moon-sipped calculus
of the lovers' electrical circle casting reverse shadows

Running along your mouth of the celestial volcano
lips of your magnetic riverbank law of the owl parliament
A riddle of waterfalls behind your smoking eyes
your face in the flower's renegade pistil
A waterfall of riddles where we bathe in hooded robes
of the harmonic alphabet

Each moment I begin the enigma

suspended magnets cry an oral torch

The river of mock-calculus will never bleed

a mask of kerosene liqueurs

Humor for our kiss and a nail

A nail matching the emblemic fires

at the cloud rigor above the stars and skies

with the tongue of death

or a forest of eyes pulled from

Lautreamont in another delirium

the oblique censor of confrontation

    and our masks

lit by night: small oracle of the winds

visible covenant of invisible flesh

The lambskins hung up before the fire

Retracers

"...that we must determine to *unify,*
re-unify, hearing – to the same degree that
we must determine to *unify, re-unify, sight.*"
(Andre Breton, *Silence ∂'Or)*

The accident, just as answers have no answers, is no
accident; whereas dreams catapult the silent orgasm of the
storm, the woman drifts with fertile lips earthbound in perseids
of mummies' hearts, oneiric lips of prisms reflect carnelian trees
& deserted tendrils of the encephalon, lips of spine visible
now only by her breast-shaped eyes.

The thread of mountains is a stream of sponges from which
a man emerges sweating birth in blindness bound by mastodon
tusks to a raft of redwood trunks ferried by panthers & wrens.
Amaurotic ecstasy transprobes the molten vector of this man of
tuberous amulets ascending with spontaneous constellations
of fertility into the exosphere now hailing arms of electro-
magnetic delirium. The end of paradoxes suffers hermetic
implosion the color of serpents when on fire.

As if reading his mind she utters, "Light may be
achromatized by joining prisms or other refracting bodies
which have opposite dispersing power," & produces a mural of
ballerinas. The link appears reinforced by the image of the
double & the wearing of masks. Love-rafts of the dragonfly, a
window of no dimensions has sent its bear wings awaiting
green shadows of hypnosis filtering the top floor where you are
a new wound on tournaments; the window repulsed by full
moons that turn to quarters beside the wrench of gloved
stairwells. Technically drowning, the dis-embodied that gape at
freedom through the ceiling of forks humble their leg irons
before the lovely skin is weaved, injected, coerced by the
solitary cry of geese flocks the two figures punctuate with the
cinema of door smoke, as spiders clothe the pending figure of
(Maps) with emotions like a gaunt train erotically tracking the
spectrum of ocular skies negating his voice whose carnal
fountain ejects abnormal life of enslaved phenomenon & peels
from her hair of milk grapefruits we squeeze of passacagliac
opiates bathing the crack of God as only god can be cracked on
a ladder of carrots scaling the abyss of lungs:

"Axils of camouflaged memory," he stutters . . . . his voice
now comes from a crater filled with telescopes radiating the
choreography of mermaids bandaging flutes harmonizing with
his statues as "sweet breezes of your eye of flesh allay the
bacteria of my heart's resonance of castration with anchors still

my hand that cannot freeze without the ink of flame kindling octaves of crescent choruses of feather," as the crater disappears, then reappears in the woman's empty arena as she composes the whiplash of reticence.

The circle of stars on the marble floor of the palladium led me to believe our embrace, after years of in one entrance of arcane dances and out the *potential* other, was no mere locking of bodies but a supernal translation of the combinatory forces discovered within magnetic wood when surrendering to fire.

First impressions, I thought.

We declared the impossibility of release from one another we flamed so with the acknowledged ingress of pluritonic uproar and became our own ashes, as all Great Arsonists realize as the *urgency of the nascent spirit*, and our own magnanimous phoenix, jewel-eyed as if crying its first and last tear, of glorious fury exploding through the ice ceiling with such abnormal convulsions of our fluid wings into the visible night's cyclorama of hypnotic crystals, a world that might have been the dream of some geometrician mad with infinity . . . I was petrified with surprise, to say the golden least, to find myself, in an instant, alone on the marble floor catching, from the other side of the palladium, this fiery glance from a passing woman I am positive of encountering (in meromorphic storm?) elsewhere.

I'm positive, I thought; I've sustained types of foot-frostbite but never diamond slippers.

Do ghosts have a right to bear ARMS?

My kneeling to closer inspect the circle of stars caused the neural arch enigma of the century. The discovery of night by a babe is comparable but salivic, I thought. Why would anyone leave this transducing amulet, with its window into the mystery, behind except if dropped by a nervous thief?

Without hesitation, I fished this etheric preternatural sculpting of the universe beyond the universe up into my hat, adjusted it carefully upon my cranium and, to blend with the wild architecture, sallied before a catenary mirror for hours where I've yet to encounter my image.

The sacred kiss of the moon's core   offers me a hand of
silence
and a tear to wipe my eyes with   at the rainbow's incision in
the night for the wing of stares

In the unlimited courier   in guns' formulas   the treasure of
this open wing   in the lost chamber that windows   links of
a red bull
charge into the light of snapped wheels

Much wider than the monastery   hiding an erostatic cure of
gems
More complete than a sewn mirror
Precise in its defining   the threaded chants   shedding from
angels' addresses of iron fur
From the stone guillotine magic reigns

Let me turn   a liquid horn   from the markswoman of
energy into litmus meteors   torn from   the stairwells of
your waist
Let me turn   the hour of the quail   into a sun-worship tribe
pulled from   the ink legs of outer swamplands

Wings have broken into sulphur   my eye upon your bleeding
buckets of perried moons

The pearl that is the orchid's intrigued harmony of glass
The calm violence of the rose   the antennae of the light from
the ankle of Andromeda
with the owl farming   for directions   from the ale of signs
and no hostages for storm coffee   or offers of sublime flesh

STRIKE Hour!

       In a matter of days the fever broke.
Curiously enough, every mirror in the house did also. "We
are reminded of the centipede with scythe wings." The
geometry of the hours interred to give this idea its corpse will
be our sole avatar of consideration. All those whose veins
swell with the new moon's liberative phase, gather to the
center. (No one moves). Ahh . . . . well, more room for me.
Those with arthritic tongues please produce 12 sheep. (No
sheep). No sheep? . . . . (searching papers) . . . . After all,
this is a study of imaginative powers, descriptions of the
flaming cup without its charred hand . . . . (finds question).
Is there any objective encounter we've over-looked or altered
without a reasonable show of hands? (No hands).

       The forgotten supper occulted in the
spiral wings remained as the moss of fire the wild chorus
dreams. Rose architorture, columns equal to planet
entrails witnessed by witches' phlegm, needled the inactive
diamond-chariot to advertise clean black strokes at

medieval dawn. In contrast a balloonist argues she never murdered the shoulder flask of opportunity. We've met and have relieved the bus to the hanging of sheepskins of its life-duties. Scissors acted like children when the ensemble, cringing with meninxian laughter, held silk knots in another universe. What glory remains!

By looking in the well the harp found its key surrendering on a chanting path of swollen crickets known to hermaphrodites. Clothed by your tongue, a magnet beginning to dance ran the gang of prescription lobsters only if the function of corners started with a halt (a group of circles which hunts for a living always pulls an automobile out of a bell-jar), when the lightning wig washed ashore for the rabbits to play with. The deserted universe brought me small tins of ichor to place at the walls of her image when the sun inflicts a swan with transparent igloos.

The impossibility of iron and the mystery of spice, an axis off the compass like syphilitic prayer in the REM of the burning figurehead, speaking the warrior language of living tissues, transforming the whistling hooks, the tonal Cheops and the personal milk clock the active gun-runner sprays with earth.

Hardly becoming wind-sticks to the thigh of captive flesh,

the Hyadean attack sends the neuronic passim to the

centers the mischievous vampire sleeps with elsewhere.

Act 1

scene 1:

A distant group of people assembled awaiting dawn.
The signal of four screams brings the earth's rotation to Kirby's
Colossal Elephant (video diagram) flaming like the rising sun
(silences) as three silver bullets become apparent hanging
above a fountain (turning invisible). The chameleon slowly
descends and the bullets become fireflies (ancient music).
A robed/masked Woman appears and a cannon explodes to her
movement. A masked dummy flies from the cannon (offstage),
landing in her arms. From both sides of the stage come (l.)
hooded figures pushing a mirror and (r.) a blind xylophonist.

scene 2:

Beneath a marble tent –

> *masked woman:* "I have lanced love and
> love has found my eyes."

> *(no light):* "...black as the pre-egyptian
> knife of the flaming magnet of
> tears."

An elevator shaft is dimly lit. Next to this stands the Robed
Woman, the mirror, and a statue nodding lights into the
audience. A picture of nuns being hung from camels is vague
between the ions and super ions dispersed by opposite wind-
machines. (The audience feels this strength through two
machines at the back of the theatre and through music
played (cries?)).

To be left in mysterious form:

(1) Robed Woman   (2 actors)

(2) mirror (yellow lights)   (2 knife-throwers)

(3) statue (nodding lights)

(4) Guillotine (red lights)

    scene 3:

    A charged woman is being hanged while the audience
enters. One by one the 12 jury members leave their chairs as
the moon's cycle of revolutions-at-hand begins (in each seat:
stethoscope, sewing machine, 4 small curtains, object deluxe,
peripheral anvil, my wife, corneas every shape, size, etc.,
whales, artists, phonographs, tomatoes, cloth).

Federal Quartz

First the issuance where we fall through the cursed owl-heart
In cro-magnon welds of the uterus
As we sip our champagne flesh
more Danish, much darker than the mystery opening the slide
rule of your heart

You have the mind of a terrorist
as beautiful and green as the shadow outside

Figures of crystal, figures the shapes of the future,
wrapped into my veins that call above a twilight dream
of the nitrogen intake
where your slippers walk me to those stars

My habits are your twisting knives of olmec tearing
as deep as the private scalpel
of the figures we embrace
in onyx thermonuclei
envisioned in the rivers' glove of memory

we sierra in our opal night between the ovaries

known in a wink to the deep blue sea

when our kiss is equal

to the double-cross about your lips of mercury and wind

Figures of habit, as shadowy as they may seem grown against

the pelvis

where we divide the flames

of our photograph altered through the kiss of temper

bleeding in the wine of memory given your wings

of toucan-wolf

mittens growing my placard of sun worship

Byron Baker

Una Sull'atra

Of all the screeching fortresses allied in silence
Violent silence, willed by the tickling
and fed by the terminal ghosts to the heart-cavern of moon
inventing thorns to an accordion at unknown intervals

The moist fingers of sciomantic wind will embark
Souls within the telescope of endless proportions
I keep at the edge of our companion the mirror of physics
The mirror that presupposes a tilted ocean of flesh
Flesh that would be the stalk of centuries and candle for
                              the animals I become

I possess and enlist a magnetic ice of the skins to hurl the
predator
by the crescent hand to onyx stimuli
I possess the mouth of solar Jacinta
We reach on simple tentacles disturbed
by corsets of angels with the power of swim-fire onyx stimuli
I posses rivulets of the great blind owl
when we dance the forged figurines to absolute zero
and we bite our nervous lip in boulder-strewn desire

and once again pull the gowns from the crack in the sky
sandstone ritual past your inner mouth
to the cores of the sacred when we will these stars
to fuse onyx stimuli

Each moment I begin the enigma

suspended magnets cry an oral torch

the river of mock-calculus will never bleed

a mask of kerosene liqueurs

Humor for our kiss and a nail

a nail matching the emblemic fires

at the cloud rigor above the stars and skies

with the tongue of death

or a forest of eyes pulled from

Lautreamont in another delirium

the oblique censor of confrontation

and our masks lit by night:

small oracle of the winds

visible covenant of invisible flesh

the lambskin hung up before the fire

The Morphometric Call (in The Region of The Heart)

A trumpet, a lunar wing, a magnet, a broken eye

With only the cobalt lights in graduating arcs

With only the salutary glare the tigress propels

With only the wound healing the scorched shadow

With only the soliloquy of birds within the charms

With only red seasons to plant the germ soul

With only black triggers in wet laughing cures

With only the invisible arrows of ancient orbs

With only magnetic shawls to give me breath

With only the lagoon's foliage to spark new nights

With only the collapsing wing of the cleft eyelid

With only the sea, the mob, the amniotic kiss

With only the wedges tilled by the window's cousin

With only masks exploding as secrets live

With only cherishable leaves in tuning forks

With only the angry cup in the shallow pond

With only a single tooth to grind a single nerve

A trumpet, a lunar wing, a magnet, a broken eye

Caustic wheels from the thorn of planets

Trumpet of the underworld sheets burning cups

on the diagonal railway made of nuns' teeth

A lunar wing as the dynamo plummeting the steam of
thought

A magnet in the fields of celebration of invisible
science

The wealth of a broken eye raining the hyacinth
bedding

Of ultra-violet gypsies unplugging the rectory

In the cemetery of soaring lances

A trumpet, a lunar wing, a magnet, a broken eye

The Solvent Mask of the Cornea

By no means would an animal death come to the emetic passion
when the dreaming flame and gold triskelion find an unisonous
field, the waterfall of charm shall unfetter sublime tones
Inert tones provoked by the shield of reverie's chill,
succinct tones of marble horse-hide, omnitones of my humours
as fresh women caressed within accelerated vessels halting
planetarily to bid exit the jeering poetics of her guns:
vital laser sail, soluble cries lost to the breaches

Fruitive sand cast from dreams a metabolic sense divides thru
rain caustic as perfume combing the goose not with sudden
orbs but candles with the negated wind of cranes liquid in the
Mighty Gusts Seeing the diagonal housing of sight, a field of
giant iron more reminiscent of cashmere than attempts of
ornicide
Giantess, giant feeling — feeling, spur of the rising glen,
pigment lost thru (and thru) faunal exploration in floral
theories

On the divan your disappearance enlarges while settlers
immersed in involuntary shadows pull the blankets from the
skies bridled to the ear of attractive bursts
What the swollen breast can feed the swollen eye can insurrect
what the glans of time can reproduce the fibers of chance
put to sleep
what every common shell drowns the imagination drowns
four out of five
acts of the flame what continents are to flavor, twilight of the
last oppressive curls like the maddened captive locked in an
invisible cell with an invisible key that a corporeal life raft
relativized with an invisible kiss

11.

Sea of coats, pay no attention to what I toss to you
my greetings are merely a composite wrath of harmony,
a ridding of the feasts encountered at will where you and I, sea,
have built our catapult with panels of flesh
Linger there, your ripe voice lisps hysterically fuscous and
fevered where the nickel of the scented harbor praises the
music of the knife
Dine to your depths bringing us back the slippery teeth
never suspected of sustaining elegant tides and her embrace
in the dolphin's laugh
Until now, projection of your film remains a mystery

Sea of coats, pay no attention to what I toss to you,

only rigid shapes are visible at your radial borders and this's just where you awaken

Sea of coats, diving in the heat like blind miners, pirate of my nerves, recall the tariff miraged between your pupil, formidable wall

Chants flaming with nitrogenous hands, clay tract of our calcium traits make croppings of jet-stream an arrow's libidinal rite as far as the welcome-mat painted on the tip of the spring of the chromosphere

Sea of coats, diamond mummy of the infant kiss, thalaris of the resurgent moon seasonally bitten by overt shadows, shadows violently neutral like the sirenic magnet, shadows quenched with alert radiation, all liquid and light, her love,

shadows within the madder violet mound erased by snow, all red and gaseous, her tongue,

shadows wedding without discourse, her mask

through passages that sleep in dreams

     a single flame of soil accepts lattices carved every morning

     phantoms raise their celtic lips

through passages that sleep in dreams

     recital of alembic quarters drill to the deafness of earth

     and in a laden chest the coasts shake hands between

jungles

through passages that sleep

      through the disappearance of a world eye of cordial

moss like a cup in dreams

      when minor rings re-establish the casket of priests'

      shrunken sense and etheric *convictions* allowing my

      senses the ennui of avid shock with the faintness of a

      wrecking crew encompassed with salt harmonics by the

      planetary caw

through passages that sleep

      on ladders the flaming woman inters with telemantic

      movements creasing aural planes available in a lash

At last the stranger to rope finds its meaning through dialectics

of the eye

Lunar terrace, eternal axiom of the milky pulse, whose calm has

been demanded to hide under its own bed, and when emerging

for an instant is only a mirage of fire or air

Lunar terrace, celebration of the alchemy of foreign suns,

ceremonies of dormant senses in the chorus of passion,

direction of human enormity

Lunar terrace, council of triggers darkened by shadows about

the flaming night, vaccine of love's eye, I become the compass

hydrologics never suspected in the hollow of the gliding circuit,

welded by erotic twins of glass

Solar quadrangle, phantoms of the phenom, chart of radiant
scissor-like women surrounding the moist temper in the cogs of
earth, eager lips stealing kisses from the rustling heavens
breaking the laws of sand
Solar quadrangle, entrance to acrobatic flesh of your lion ice,
put to the test of deeper burial into werewolves behind coarse
eyes of a shaved lake sprung from traps
Solar quadrangle, swept throat of mirror, click of the water
pistol, sight curled away in viscous ratios we will drink as tears
younger than the desert
of your forbidden fiber

Swimming in the Buffalo

All through the nights flesh had abandoned my dream
with the cool ankle of owl a storm kneading one last kiss-sight
Portrayal younger science keeps below an ether necklace
torn by the light, shadow torn into pieces

From

ATLATL VIGILIA

Ante Bellum

for the Absolute Constants

Cerulean knives exit the shadow hoop
on the vast reef of secret instants robed
with the hidden gown of deaf leaves
The libran net of love enigmas desires' lotteries
from the luminous seas to the bermuda of your eyes'
        jaguar wing
Open-mouthed to the x-ray cup full of coiling moons

    +   +   +   +   +   +   +

The shadow of fire is gravity is obsessed with the shadow
        of ice

    +   +   +   +   +   +   +

At the edge of the calendar a new season kills its beak
Epochal shears of bamboo spirits protrude from the heart
Crowned with blood silk from the equator's feather telescope
Not star clusters but lost panes bring me
        refreshment from the winking cedar
In this way at night my shadow is still visible

At the edge of the calendar ghosts make your new hat

From the erotic folds found between girandole atoms

Twelve belts of linen affixed dialectically like chills

   with the manito tongue-charms of intimate rays

turn back into themselves like the turtle of signs

   and the whistles of light

In this way at night my shadow is still audible

  when the flaming storm unmasks the color of echoes

The Great Mists of Earth

Anchors have been severed worlds apart where lethal beauty
sings
From the hyperblindings beyond the dreaming flash lyre
Rotative as the silent eggs of water talismans unexplored
In the eyes heated by a choir eclipse
In the eyes
Dark gloves hold the hammer by winding its throat
In the eyes of memory thrown from its balcony of reflex
navigation
All the spider-cells in the angered quartz museum
In the eyes spun from the moons of other light
In the eyes *attack through passion*
     my first kiss with the skies spills
In the eyes of black wine or blood of fission
     casting white shadows through a paladin's
     empty sword
In the eyes of flight to the prisms in nights of the body:
     —Optos
     —cenece akur lite

　　　　—lynx

　　　　—Etx' qlnt' ftx'Rtn

In the eyes breathing eroto-magic of equatorial signals

In the eyes closing in a moth

In the eyes changing in the plasma wind circuits

In the eyes behind the eyes of the triceratops

In the eyes captured with the ghosts of the phantasm

In the eyes of sound elevators the surprise marmots plant

In the eyes of the dark stars in the pouch of revolt

In the eyes of mirror sewn in sleep

In the eyes causing the birth of myths coupling

　　　with the sea beyond the sea lemma

In the eyes shot out in a graveyard protecting owls

In the eyes' secret liaison with glass-tongued replicas

　　　of the coffee grinder's closet arrows

In the eyes predicting the past and future exofuse

In the eyes of bone rivets falling at my feet

In the eyes recharged with the waterfalls of space

　　　and the first banquet with the stars

A Show of Hands

for Alice Farley

The shore beneath your diamond ritual climbs the fountain
I am bleeding from with cranes, my shells, of the great seal

Cq'olos, Bhtr'mxy, Fortu'qxe, A'mkq

There are chariots giving my heart its swollen stain
Just as there are gallows embroidered with manic armaments
But the genesis of emblems that holds the menagerie of storm
                              within my blood nacre
Suspends from the golden solicitant of isotopic layers impulsive

Lmt'akrtl, Sqoln'cr, M'curu'sh, Sknt'wlgr

The point beyond hidden cities forestalls the science of love
Where the great-masked-terrors have fallen from your eyes
To be worn about the waist as the bow-goblet coral scar
My bodies band to touch the pullen lair
And extracted notes   on an infinite   treasure-seer

Tlrq'snto, Awtr'ttsq, Lpq'trsor, Kqlto

From the ethernal tarmac in flaming vestiges

A palpitant room of scalar rings bites the sibylline knife

A sign not unlike the black hole socket of beauty

Nor the imagination shield at the dawn of assembling mirrors

On these nights in the personage of melanic winds

The tears of blood invoke seizures cast from sleep

                              and the bacteria of the senses

What were once called stars shall always take

                    human form

When the beauty and the beast are mapping love

Nerval's Lobster

We meet unnerved by flaming glass
kissing the antelope dreams of barbaric satellites
on railroad tracks that are my bed
Light blossoms in kinesic spirit
the ageless spark sets adrift
the axis sex lanterns through negative harbors
Marveling at hair growing from a sword
planted to cleanse the aorta of gypsum-blue
Incinerators accosting your freedom gown

The new antithesis speaks madly as the sun
as the silver timetable entrusts its violence to us
the curtained stream a breeding whorl
Risking the arm soldered to a horizon of shells
without disguise in an honey-dip of shadow
Elaboration of a greenhouse mirror like a stellar water
surrounded by these lava fields

Speech within the storm the desert offers
A stringed avenue where fences are swans
and okra chalices painting the ore mines
we sleep in to keep wet the inert masks
with sparkling sleeves of liquid torch
The high pitch of liberty in a woman
Waiting in my eyes of glistening cactus
to make fugitive the embalmer of tongues
surrounded by these lava fields

Sections of flame throw ringlets of bread
to the street roamed by sounds of foxes
A distant sun hurls a poetic spear
to the heart roamed by hooves of dreams
An arm thrusts like the phoenix from a stream
to the future roamed by dancers of foreheads
stacking dew with the authority of angels:
Volcanic whispers the formation of ice crystals and runs the
chance
of becoming the motions for an elixir to ravage empires

Carved Blinks of the Voyeur

The train stopped. While I glanced at the sign of the arrows an immaculate voice tore at my flesh which had become memory. Two "lepers" held hands (I mention leper simply because they wore placards about their forearms in the manner of jewelry), committing an unusual amount of flare for the mirror my eyes had surrounded for the past six years since arriving at this point of departure.

"Guns for the poor," a clear voice uttered from just beyond a rail lined with a wall of knives. "Arms for the struggle," again. I felt a very raw need to enact either these solicitations as they appeared to manifest or reveal, no matter at how certain intervals portrayed a lack of appellant misguidance in a projection of dreams and a wanderlust of the would-be fire myth, placing my revolver inside the temple.

Quite early in the Wolf Library, where music anthers of an imaginable world inaudible to most but collecting in the pockets of all find its premier setting, the twenty-two shelves concerning astrosciences had, in a swift cleave of reason, disappeared.

"Holy Chaldean Fertility," cried one-half of the Siamese librarian as I fanned the convulsing other (her actions were not unlike my own: limp ankles, enflamed and rapid eye movements, similar wax boxes forming outside the heart, faint exclamations of ancient worship) cold in my arms. Our revival methods were clearly beneficial as she awoke and whispered to me that "there were still crumbs in the bed of the food we partook of . . . still stains of rose absinthe . . . . we tastefully unlocked . . . . still lightning in the mirrors pouring my eyes from the moon."

All about was chaos, though none had noticed the missing shelves. "Perhaps in this region," we mused, "harmolodic occurrence might actually escape nature." As I reinvented the whispering smiths and falling stone axes from a Belgian sky in the next century, they leave me as master criminals secure warrior-patrols about a "prison of the mind," taking care to not mistake its ashes for fresh soil.

Not until the bindings of a cross my wrists are formed into were eaten away did the inquiry as to when the next last supper might begin, and whom might serve and whom might clean up. Disguises, for there is reverie, attract an intuitive basis ranging from Sqtrl'chem'tqr to the Atlantean fleets transcribing braille to the captive flesh an and voyage to the lawless sights.

Cross-reference

for Connie

With the sling of weeping fire to catapult the windless ice
The great islands prop me up in the doorwells
      awaiting the sea bed's messenger the pangolin
Sleeping in a fit of courage your bleeding abdomen
Attracts the tourmaline veils in magical cures
Like the contracting diamond-fury I am lean with
      and a solidification of caverns too opaque
Like the contractive whistle-mask sacred to jaguars
      when the cyprinid fruitions explode the planetary eye
Like the contracted deathblow disregarded by the fawn
      calling on the endemic magnets of cinenary love
To pull *from the secret speech* of dreaming the bald sky
And its eyebrows, arc-roses and earring: the x boomerang

    +   +   +   +   +   +   +

All the learned seasons split from head to toe with honey
Bring me sentry gales of open lakes of sulphur
At every turn the glaring undoes my spirit knots

Like the baited rose chair of infinite mantle
In the palm of spaces your opal tears of laughter are
the lifeline animations
Moral attraction in the muse of sorceries
Cohabits umbilical coves with maniacal chance
Tremendous chance, sphere magnetíque of the lost swamp
that has hidden its treasures like a locked eye
The walls of heaven built for the dead and the color of mud
Are shattered by the clarion will of formidable truth
in a mouth smiling underwater at goats' chess
in progress filtered through robed diagrams
in the red chaos acting as large as stools
in an evacuated hall of the crying rainbow
in my steering heart to the excited plume of moons
That robs through the reeling of potions exiting on the
window's crucial mare of light

Aqt'xlpa

I look for you behind the velocity of gloves
Behind the oceanic pulse of words that tarot the night
Between the orchestrated pillars where cliffs sway in
    the cosmetic whip of gravity
In the graveyard of seasons and carbon triangle of skulls
In the sun's backward motions and hijacked lips
Beneath your stairs of waves and hot-iron senses
In the parlors of the insane and hermetic scripts
    with hibiscus pages in eternal flower
Behind pluvial laughter of the northern lights' song
Behind the green umbrella of lion eye's blood
In a hypnotic chevron when your hand jewels sweet poisons
Beneath a fulminant wheel of tana leaves nailed to the wake of
    the crying-flame theater

I tell the elements "Each corner, each curve!"
And they tell me they too are looking for you
Behind the dreaming gates at the harvest of the winds

A Hostage in the Arms of the Honey Eaters

"An ancient record — still worse, an ancient Chinese record — of a
courtyard of a palace — dwellers of the palace waking up one
morning, finding the courtyard marked with tracks like the footprints
of an ox — supposed that the devil did it."
(Charles Fort)

"Whatever you may attempt, very few people let themselves be
guided by that unforgettable light."
(Andre Breton)

"The fragrance of glass is the handle of time."
(Jocelyn Koslofsky)

"I wanna dance, I wanna sing, I wanna hotchacha!"
(Groucho Marx)

+   +   +   +   +   +   +

By diving into sceptre pools of the mercury borealis

Great miracles fly underwater on the constellations chained to

your arson lips

You have caught my glimpse through the adrenaline swings

that become skin combed by trance in the defiant silo our veins

connect

Mystery blankets the bell language

                    to wrap you with

throughout the astronomy of bones I steal from the grass
necklace
                    for the queen of sheaths
Hidden among the lost beaks of your skinned label
and legs of wine

Helium magnesias the thought behind sprig voices of the eyes'
wax leaf
Pistols being threaded into the "silver disk" needle
like mermaids
The grave activity we are reminded of belongs to the centipede
                    with scythe wings to wrap you with
Vampiric sleep
The ceiling of pheasanta keys to the intromit nights
as the night with its cloak of nervous armor walks with its back
to us
Where optic flames like a throne on the milk of tears
lip-read the skull of seas flung from our throat to wrap you
with
The living myth to wrap you with aural levers of our armadal
touch
                    within the vector spirit
Here the magician kisses the juggler's burnoose mask of
working crime
at the intermission never acceptable to an insignia of wood
codes

in the proton breaches like the water beginning with the earth
for an ignitive sign with the elan cups pouring a gold of
language

into your iris mannequin in the execution

between the wild vines and curtains magic

fertiles

From a pelt of blue sheets formulas like water
glide from the mouth of spears great life affords
The tureen compass my coils ingest with the birds' breakings

of the mirrors to the finest energies

Each wound makes my climb to light a marriage with word
and the stigmata in full tropics of umor

    +   +   +   +   +   +   +

From the stone guillotine magic reigns

    +   +   +   +   +   +   +

Crosses sold on the cuirass poles are as hazardous as shotguns
when the hooded woman places her eye on a corpse bearing the
slogan "VANISHED LOVE" as an arcola of flame wheat
Actress in the violence of dreams
   in the gripping pampas
   in the cello's hug
And the blackened wood-wraith pulling my covers off the kelp
sky
To wrap you with an omnilateral abeng* secured
in the narwhal pulse for the gambol serenade to love's figurine

My questions eat like an electronic stallion

and the community of your science-mark of lava

The conjunction of distant flutes obeys the eel's voice

where crying statues bleed in the moon's embrace

                the hidden gem of my fluid

To wed the honey spore before the enclaves of light

I will weave piassava footwear for an angel's corpse

to remind the beauty the ocelot of the drinking sheets

of extra-celestial rumors

in sleep's mimicry of black dolphins' plateau-eloquence

in the winds' faces of the missing shadow

I remove tendons and release the flags of invisible agents

               to the Camorra deputies with our own

glass helmets with litmus meteors

    throughout the palace beneath the perfumed

           flesh of the sacred

* A cow horn whose sound carries for miles through western
Jamaica's Maroon hills, imposed as a weapon in 1517 and developed
as a look-out system in the late XVIIth century when the warrior-
languages, led by Cujo, enacted, and appropriately cried, revolt
against the attempted colonialization of their sovereign state of
being.

NOTES

Jhim Pattison (1951-2009) continues as an outstanding figure among American surrealists – a prolific poet and collagist, occasional essayist and playwright – a unique presence. It was mostly in and around Los Angeles and San Francisco that Pattison led an exemplary life of the artist; part hermit, part comet, part coyote. Though focused and largely self-sufficient, he nevertheless relished collaborating on group shows and manifestations, notably Harvest of Evil (Columbus Ohio 1983), Magnets of the Polar Horn (San Francisco 1985), The Secret Face of Scandal (New York 1986). Pattison was also a founding member of the experimental music group MalOcchio. Documents of these and many others of his works are included in the recent anthology *Invisible Heads: Surrealists in North America – An Untold Story* (Anon, 2011).

The present volume is a representative collection, much of it previously unpublished or of limited availability. The illustrations throughout are details taken from collages by the author, with the exception of page 46, *Una Sull'atra* by Byron Baker (see note below).

Notes to pages:

Cover. *Posture in an Ancient Law of Night . . .(The Last Rites of FAFA) During the Ice Age (or the Singing Reduction)*, by the author (1983).

9. "Now that those who hold our roads..." is taken from *Pueblo Gods and Myths* by Hamilton Tyler (University of Oklahoma Press 1973) and appears as the preface to Atlatl Vigilia (see note below)

9. "The Moon in the Man" appeared in slightly different forms in *The Adventures of Desiree* (Reve a Deux, 2008) and in the catalogue of Schlechter Duval's 1988 exhibition *In the O of Eros* (Oneiros Gallery, San Diego, California)

20. "The Ascent of Mary W. Shelley" is from a manuscript dated 11/84

22. "Strange Destiny" is one of several versions, this one dated 1-13-91 and imprinted with a rubber stamp bearing the words "Research Institute" and the author's address in Hollywood

32. "The circle of stars..." is from the edited manuscript with endnote: "from *The Philtre* – 1980"

42. "Act 1" is from the unpublished play *The Assassination of Neptune*, date unknown

44. "Federal Quartz" dated 5-3-83

46-47. "Una Sull'atra" was originally conceived in 1980 as a collaboration with artist Byron Baker and first published in *Invisible Heads* . . . (Anon 2011)

61. "Atlatl Vigilia," a self-published collection, circa 1990

80. "Aqt'xlpa" first appeared in *Rattler* (Los Angeles, May 1982) as the second part of the poem "In the Tradition of the Art of Inventing Characters" under author's occasional pseudonym "Geisha Sails"

ACKNOWLEDGMENTS

These works by Jhim Pattison are compiled and designed by Raman Rao with the assistance and advice of Thom Burns, Stephen Lock, Byron Baker, Richard Waara and Allen Graubard. Art Direction by Thom Burns. Additional assistance from Marsha Hartnack and Kathleen Benton.

www.ingramcontent.com/pod-product-compliance
Lightning Source LLC
Chambersburg PA
CBHW020513030426
42337CB00011B/366